Contents

1) 65 Easy Piano Songs for Kids

Mulberry Bush
Old King Cole
Hush, Little Baby
Jack and Jill
Auld Lang Syne
Hey, Diddle Diddle
Comin' Round the Mountain
Sing a Song of Sixpence
For He's a Jolly Good Fellow
If You're Happy and You Know It
Alouette
Head, Shoulders, Knees and Toes
Hokey Pokey
Away in a Manger
Alice the Camel
I'm a Little Teapot
Swing Low, Sweet Chariot
This Old Man
Amazing Grace
Drunken Sailor
When the Saints Go Marching In
My Bonnie Lies Over the Ocean
Three Blind Mice
It's Raining, It's Pouring
Five Currant Buns
Pussycat Pussycat
A Sailor Went to Sea, Sea, Sea

Hot Cross Buns

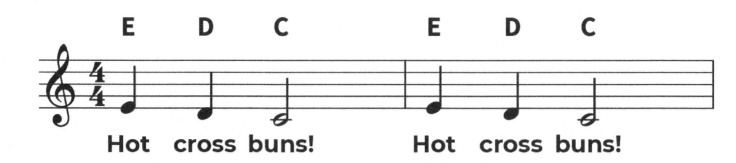

Mary Had a Little Lamb

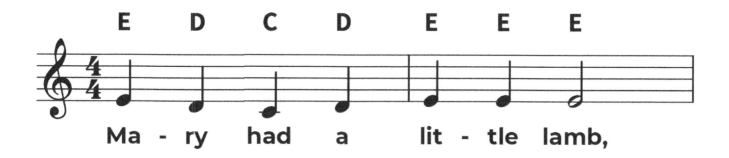

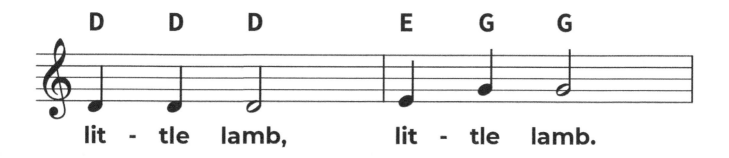

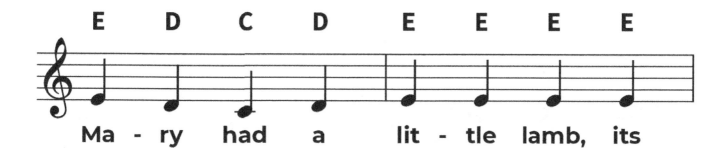

Old MacDonald Had a Farm

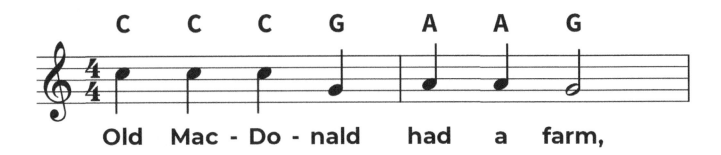

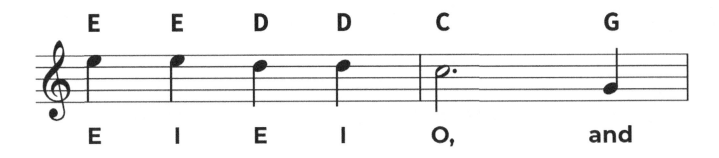

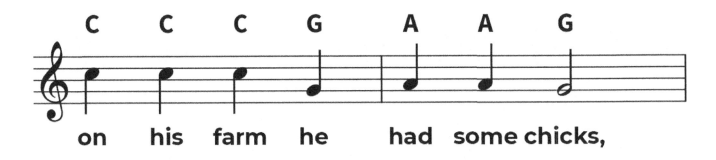

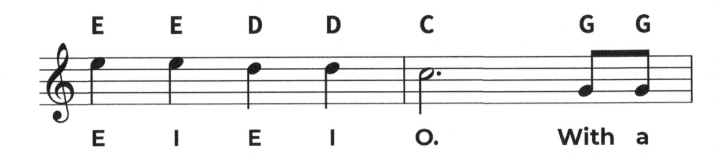

2

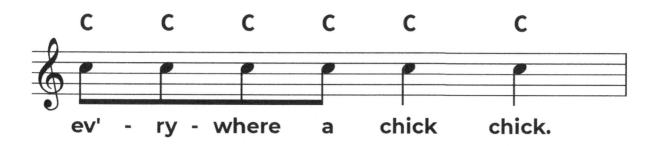

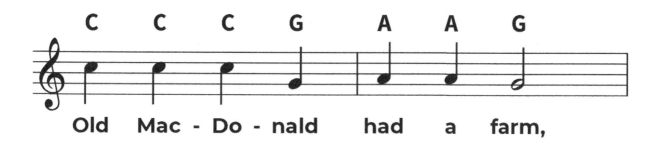

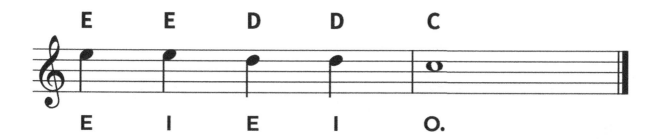

Twinkle, Twinkle, Little Star

Happy Birthday To You

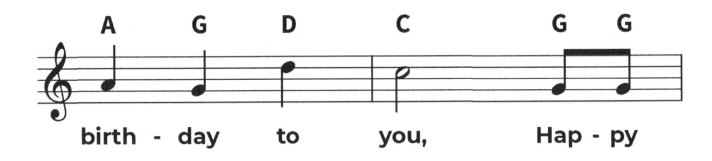

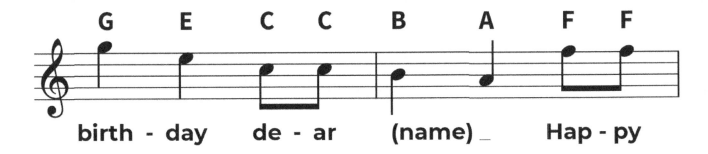

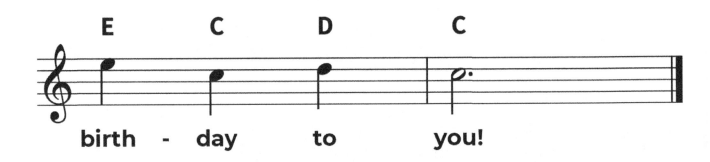

The Muffin Man

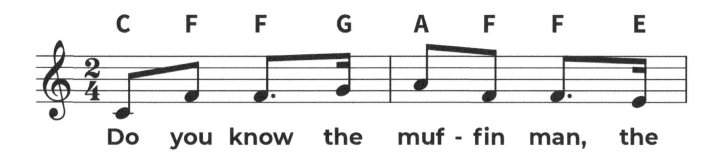

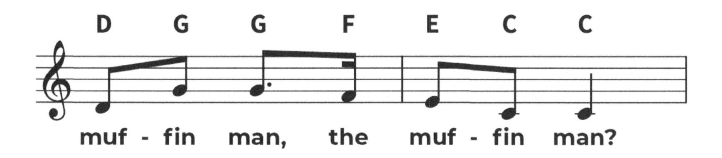

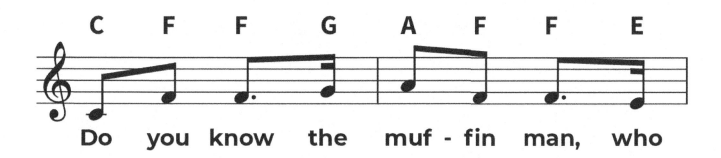

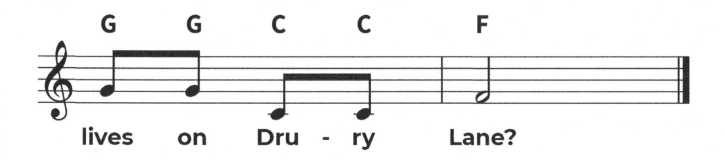

London Bridge

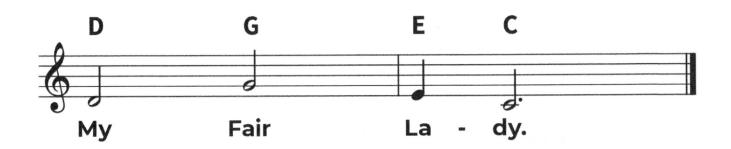

Row Your Boat

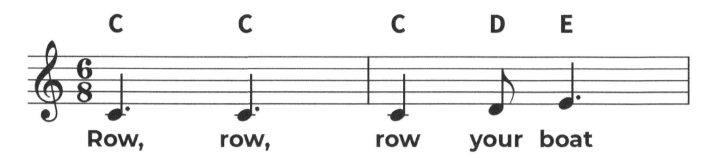

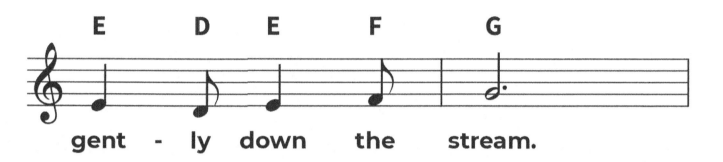

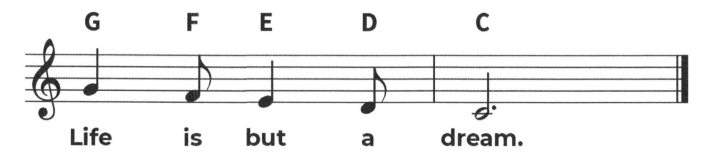

You Are My Sunshine

Frere Jacques

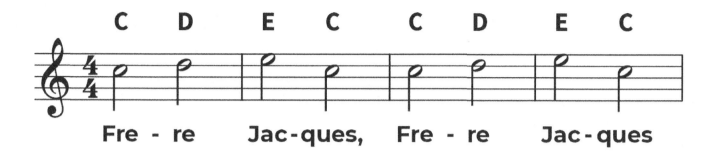

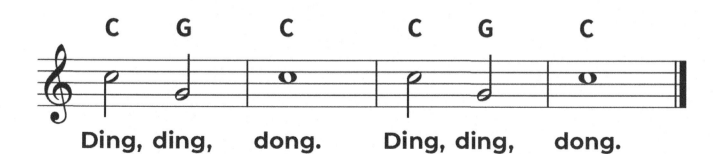

Alphabet Song

Incy Wincy Spider

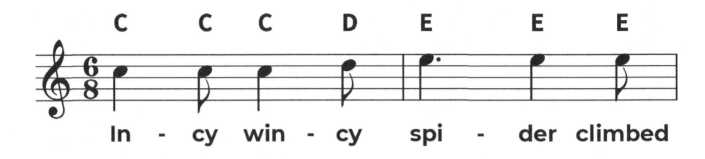

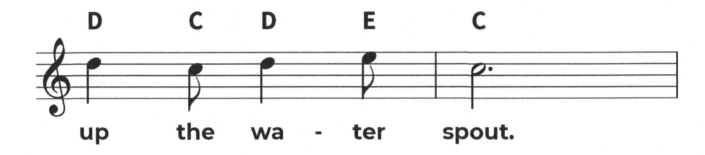

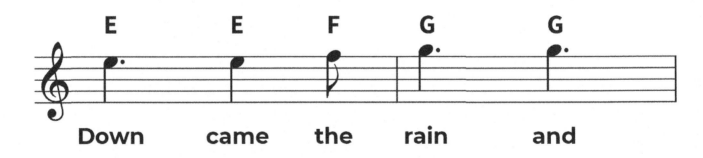

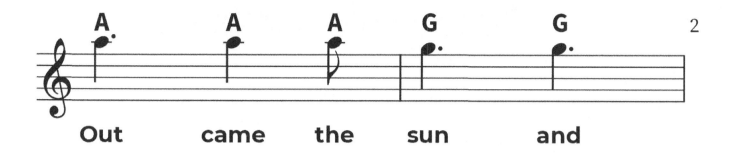

Out came the sun and

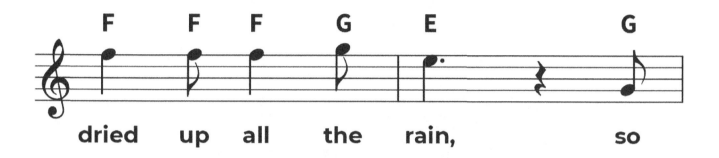

dried up all the rain, so

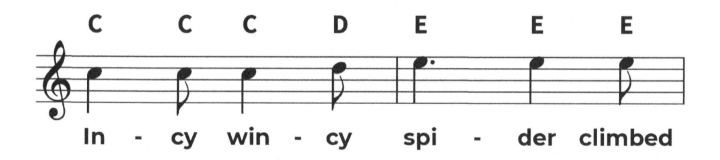

In - cy win - cy spi - der climbed

up the spout a - gain.

Rock-a-bye Baby

Wheels on the Bus

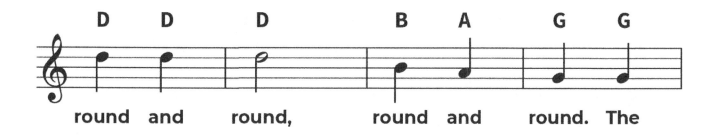

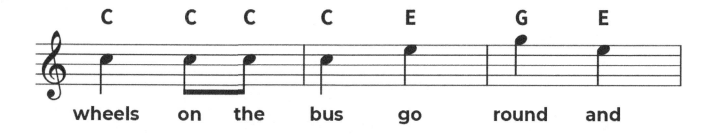

I Am The Music Man

Sing a Rainbow

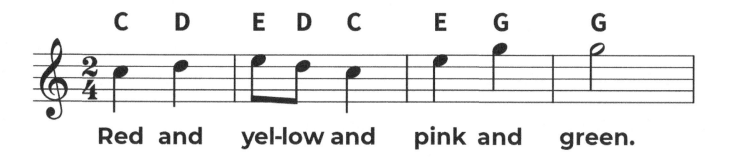

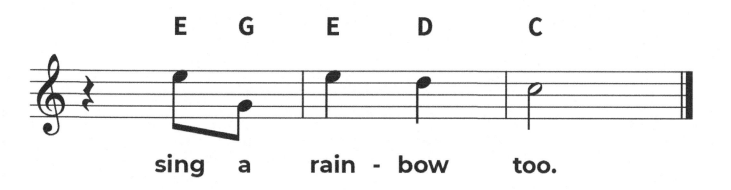

The Grand Old Duke Of York

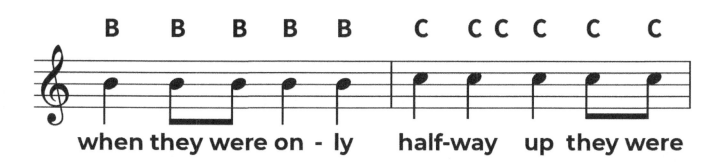

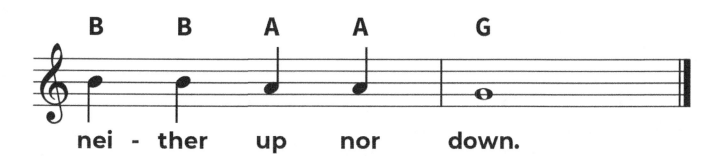

Kum Ba Yah

Silent Night

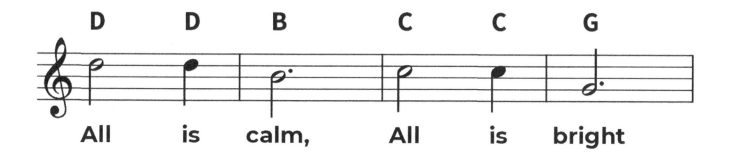

2

Joy To The World

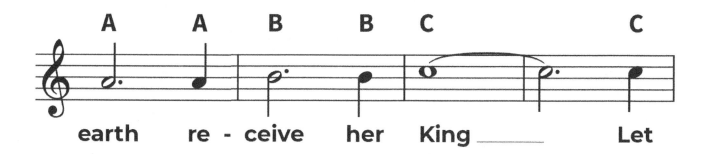

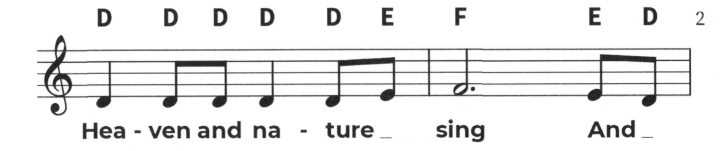

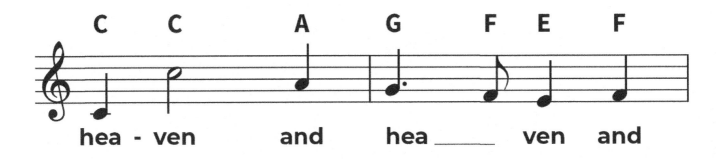

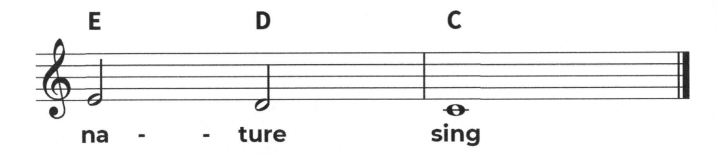

Brahms' Lullaby

Lul - la - by   and good - night,   with _

ro - ses   bes - tri - de,   with _

li - lies   be ___ decked,   ne - ath

ba - by's   sweet ___ bed.   May thou

sleep,　　　may thou　rest,　　　may thy

slum - ber　be　blest.　　　May thou

sleep, may thou rest, may thy slum-ber be blest.

Oh My Darling Clementine

dar-ling, oh my dar-ling Cle-men-tine! Thou art

lost   and   gone for - e - ver,   dread-ful

sor - ry,   Cle - men - tine.

Yankee Doodle Went To Town

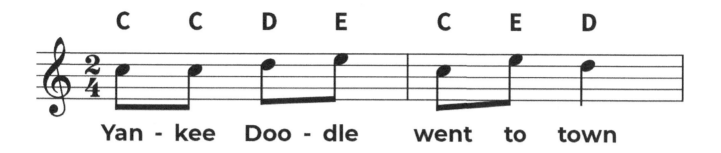

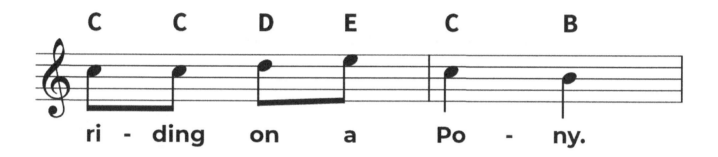

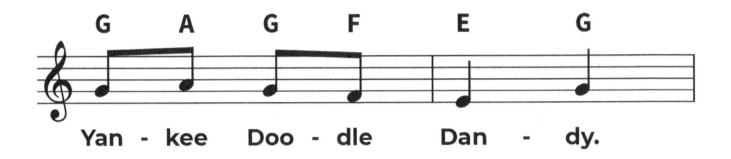

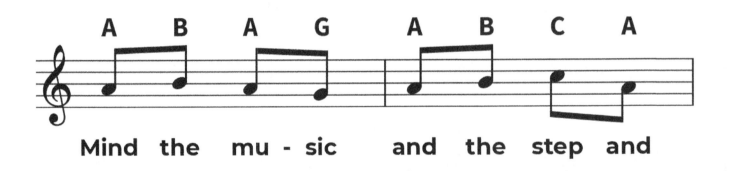

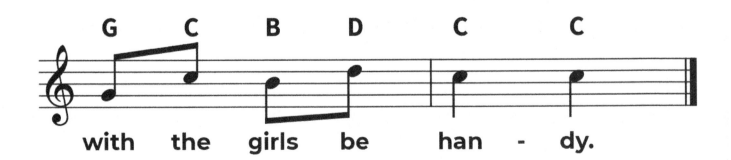

Hickory Dickory Dock

Humpty Dumpty

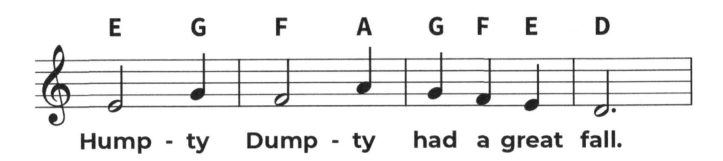

Pop! Goes the Weasel

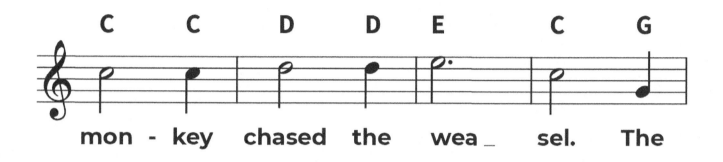

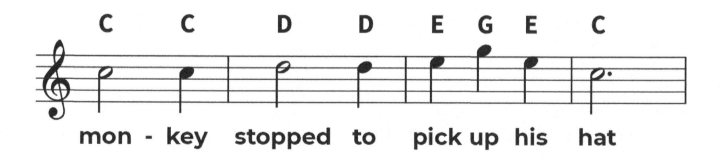

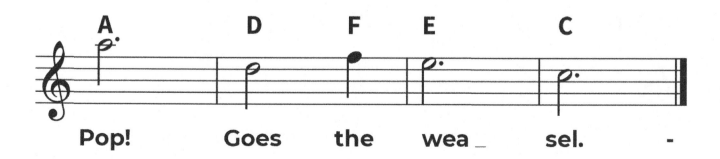

The Mulberry Bush

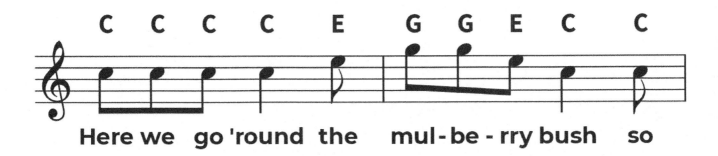

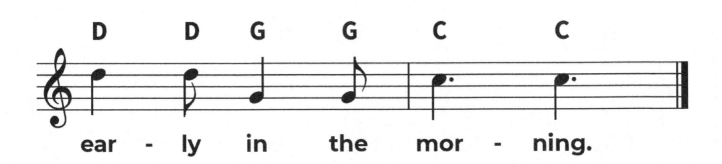

Old King Cole

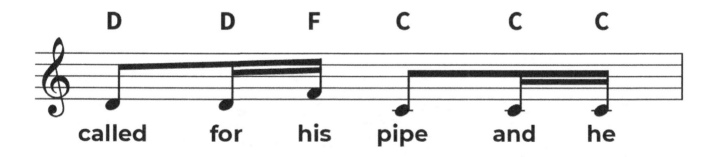

called for his fid - dlers _ three.   E - very

fid - dl - er he had had a   fid-dle   and a

ve - ry fine fid - dle had   he.   Oh, there's

none so rare, as none can com-pare with King

Cole and his fi - ddl - ers   three.

2

Hush Little Baby

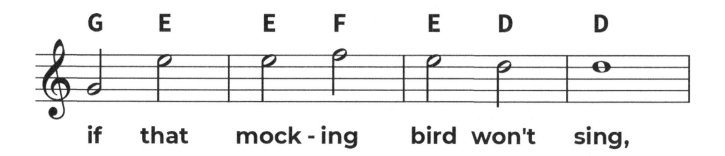

Jack And Jill

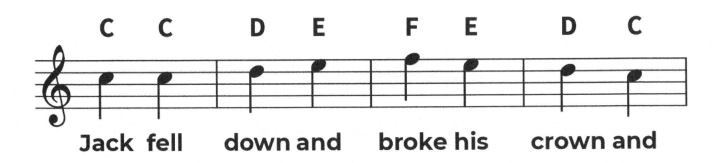

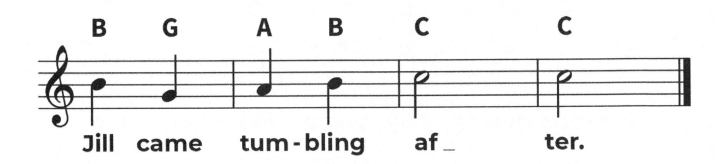

Auld Lang Syne

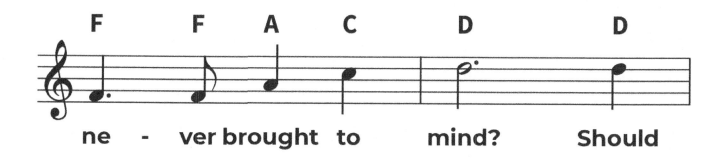

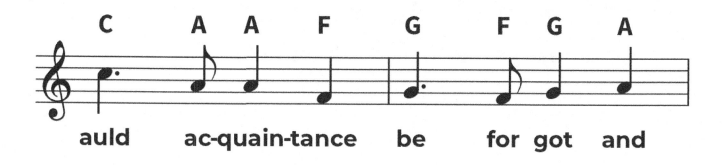

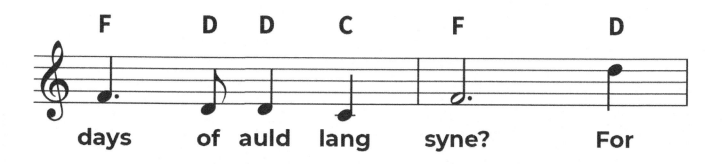

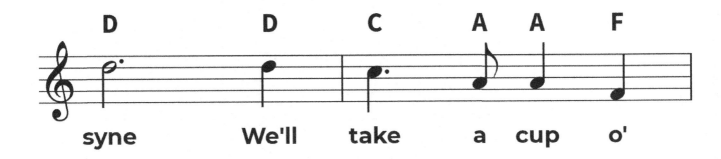

Hey Diddle Diddle

She'll Be Coming Round the Mountain

She'll be co-ming 'round the moun-tain,

co-ming 'round the moun-tain when she comes.

Sing a Song of Sixpence

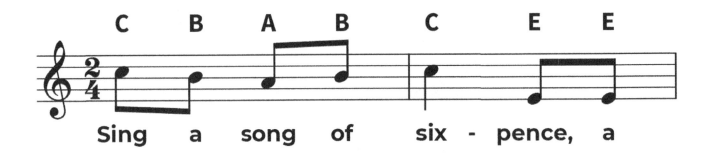

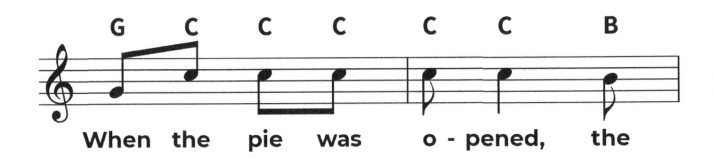

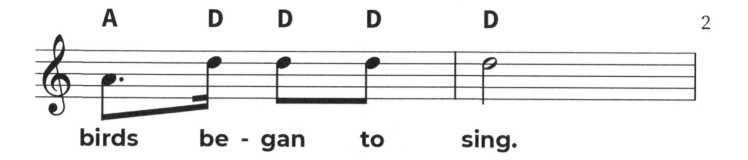

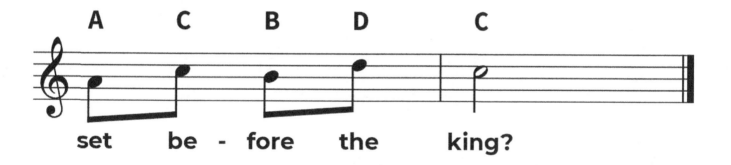

For He's a Jolly Good Fellow

For he's a jol-ly good fel _ low, for

he's a jol-ly good fel _ low, for

he's a jol-ly good fel _ low and

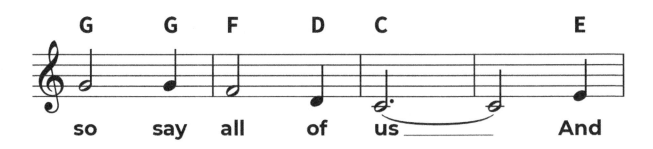

so say all of us _____ And

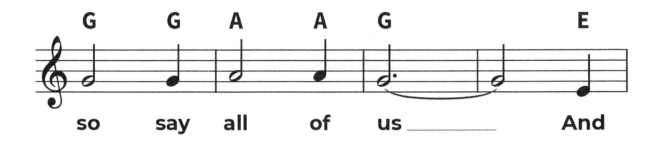

so say all of us _____ And

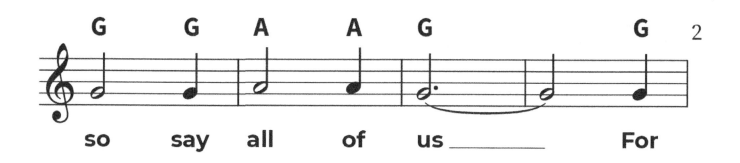

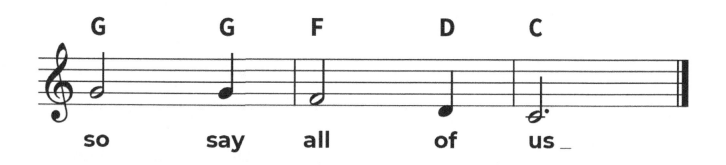

If You're Happy And You Know It

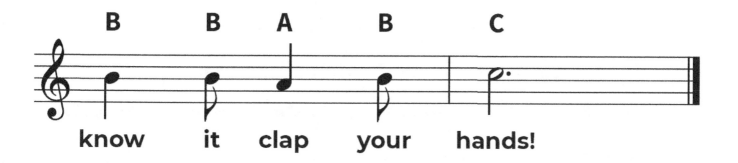

Alouette

A - lou - et - te   je te plu-me-rai.

Head, Shoulders, Knees and Toes

Head, shoul-ders, knees and toes, knees and toes!

Head, shoul - ders, knees and

toes, knees and toes _ and _ eyes and ears and

mouth _ and _nose. Head, shoul-ders, knees and

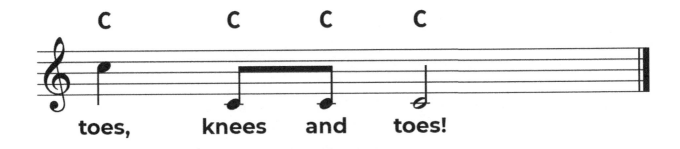

toes, knees and toes!

Hokey Pokey

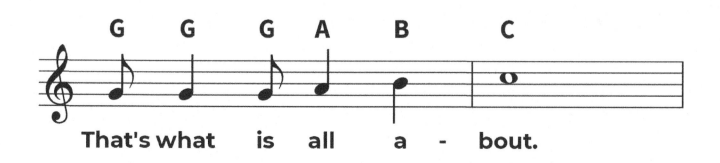

Oh _____ the Ho-key Po - key _

Oh _____ the Ho-key Po - key _

Oh _____ the Ho-key Po - key _

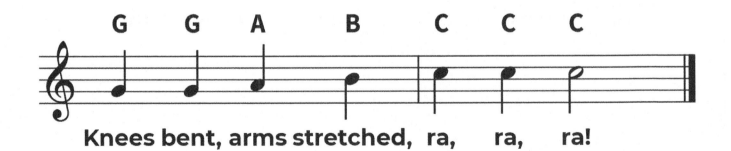

Knees bent, arms stretched, ra, ra, ra!

Away in a Manger

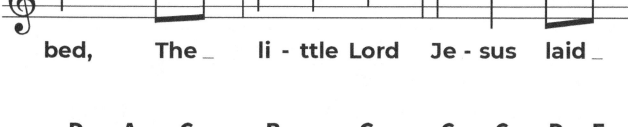

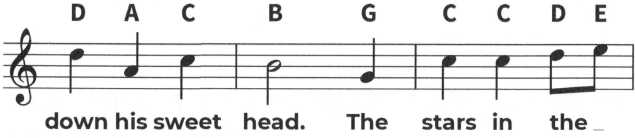

Alice the Camel

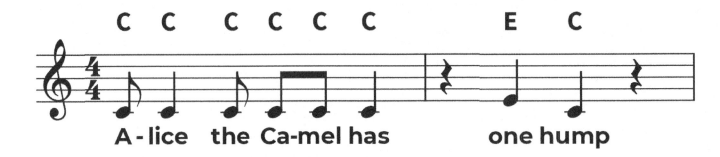

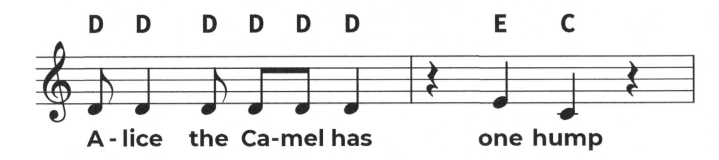

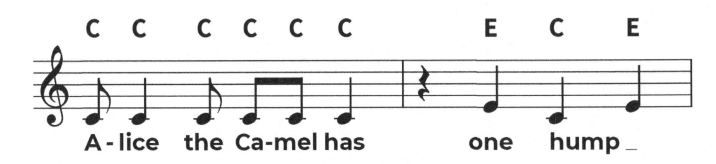

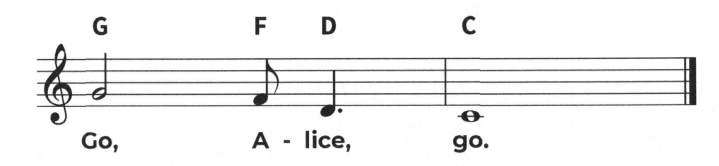

I'm a Little Teapot

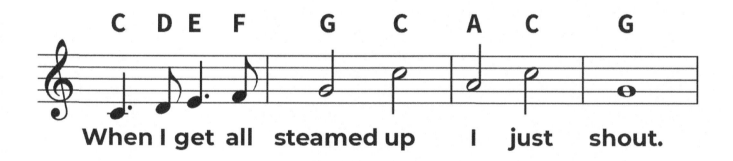

Swing Low, Sweet Chariot

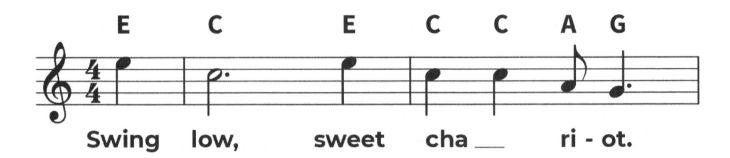

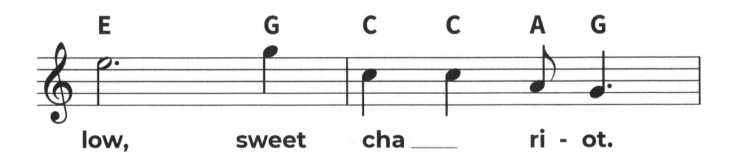

This Old Man

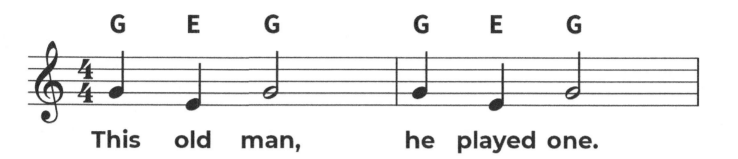

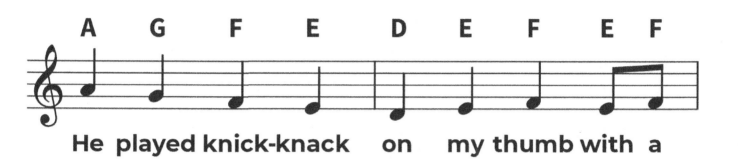

Amazing Grace

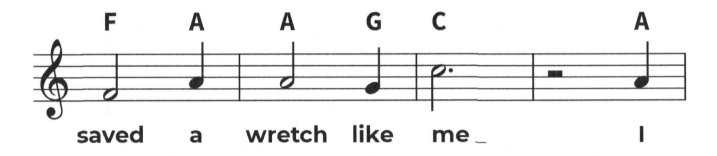

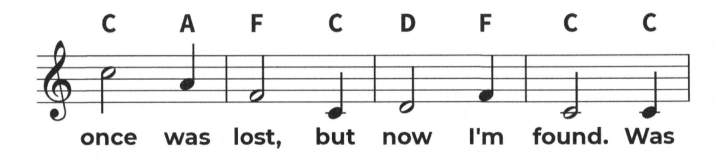

Drunken Sailor

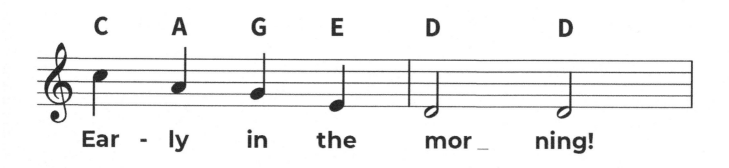

Way hay and up she ri - ses,

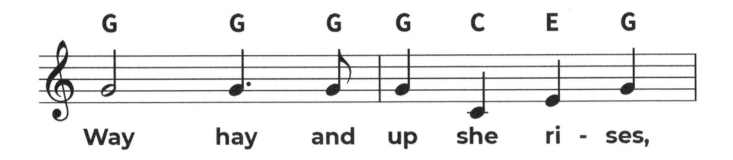

Way hay and up she ri - ses,

Way hay and up she ri - ses

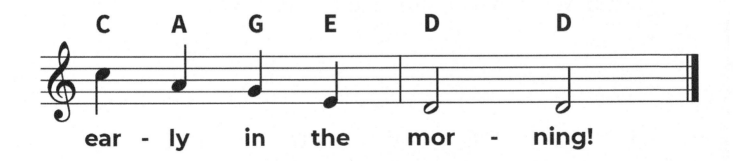

ear - ly in the mor - ning!

When The Saints Go Marching In

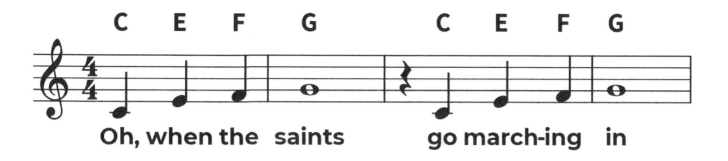

My Bonnie Lies Over The Ocean

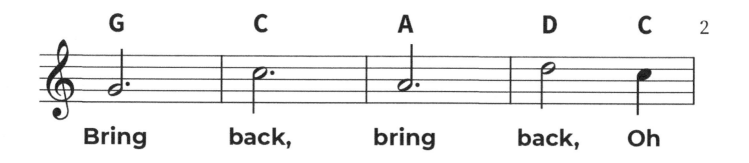

Bring back, bring back, Oh

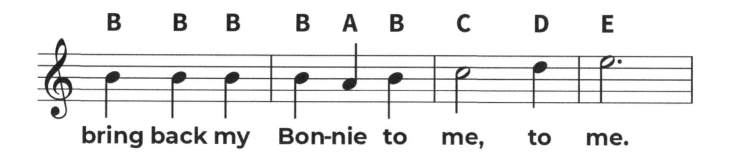

bring back my Bon-nie to me, to me.

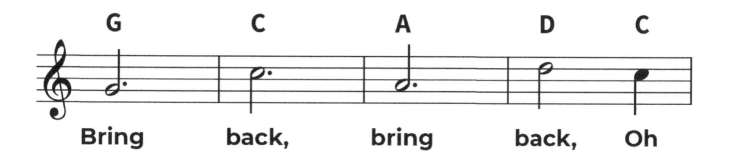

Bring back, bring back, Oh

bring back my Bon - nie to me.

Three Blind Mice

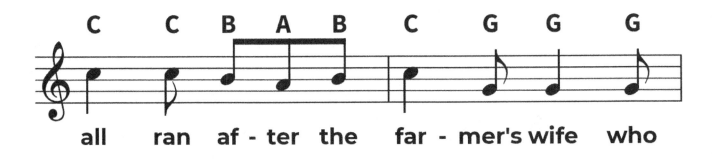

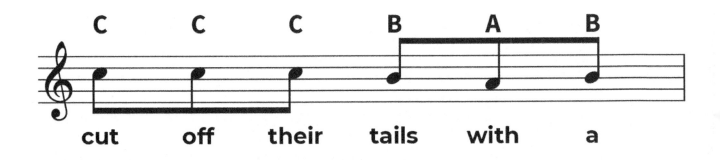

car - ving knife. Did you e _ ver see such a

thing in your life   as   three blind   mice?

It's Raining, It's Pouring

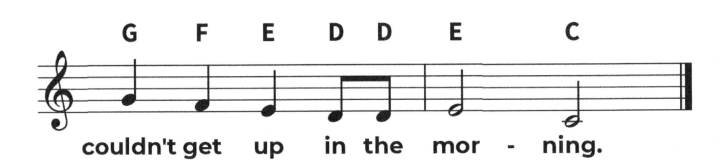

Five Currant Buns

Five cur-rant buns in a ba - ker's shop,

Round and fat with a cher-ry on top __ A -

long came a boy with a pen-ny one day,

bought a cur-rant bun and took it a - way.

Pussycat Pussycat

A Sailor Went to Sea, Sea, Sea

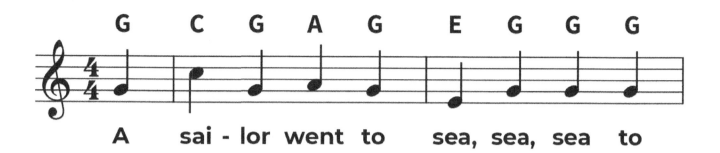

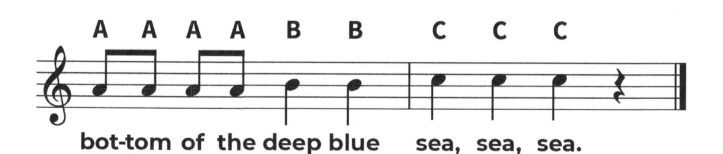

Ode To Joy

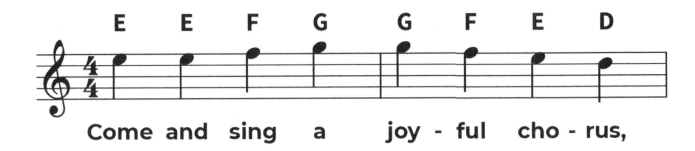

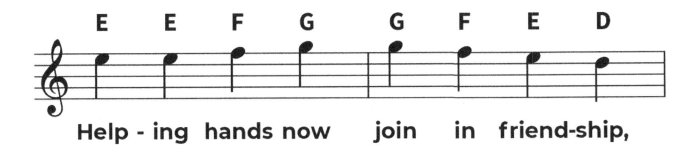

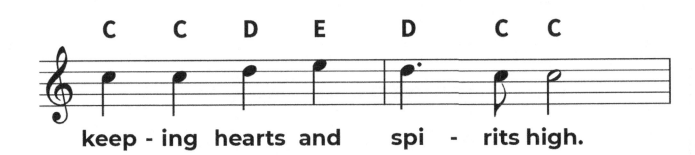

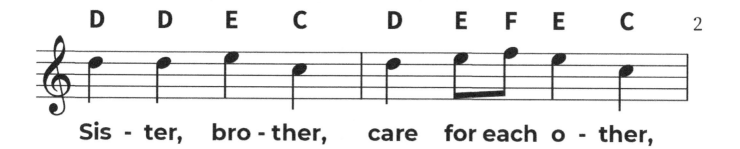

Sis - ter, bro - ther, care for each o - ther,

care for the world and keep it free.

Come to - ge - ther, sing to - ge - ther,

as a peace - ful fa - mi - ly.

Deck The Halls

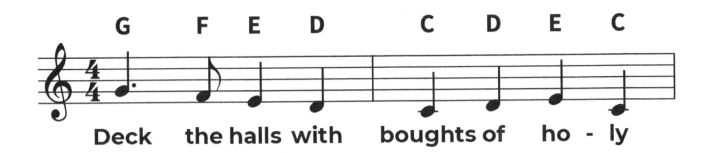

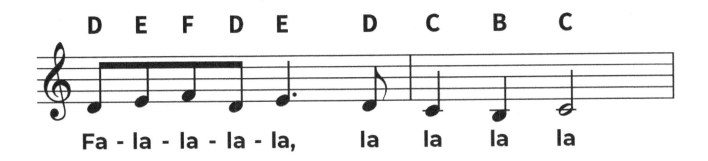

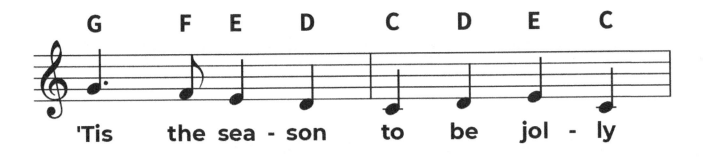

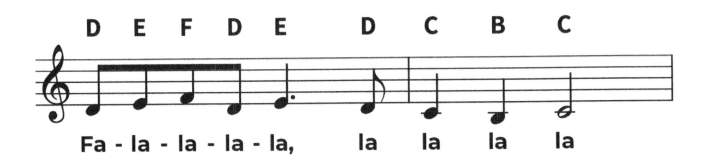

Don't we now our gay ap - pa - rel

Fa - la - la la - la - la la la la

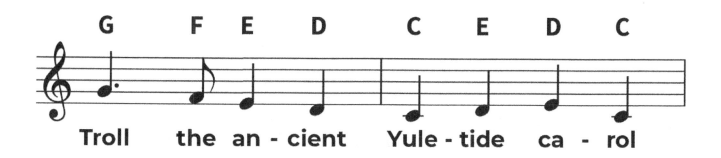

Troll the an - cient Yule - tide ca - rol

Fa - la - la - la - la la la la la

Scarborough Fair

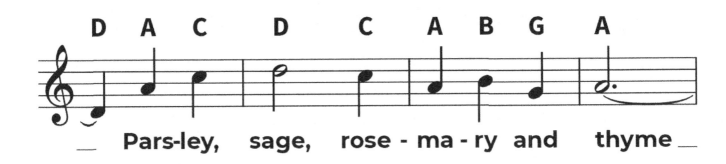

Can Can

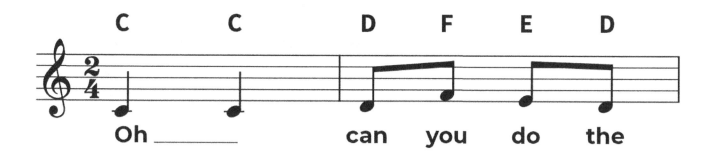

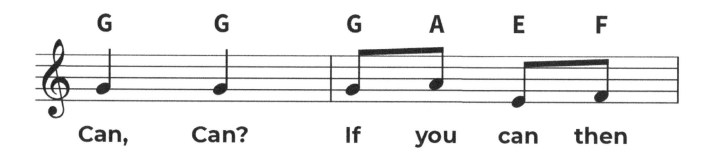

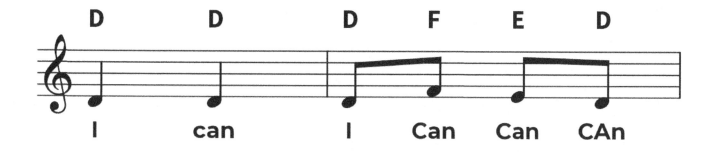

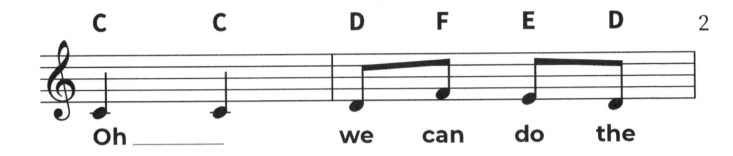

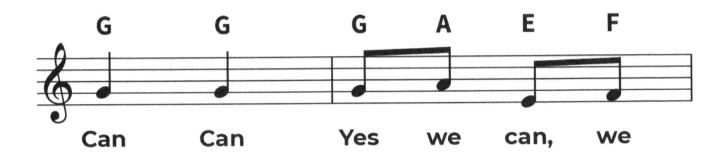

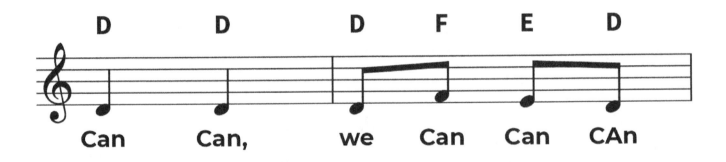

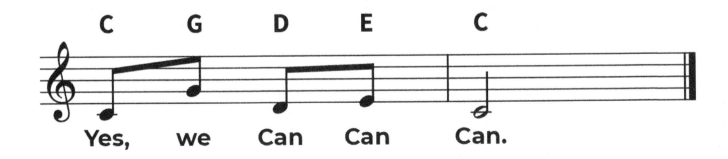

Skip To My Lou

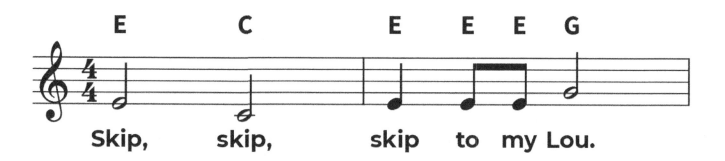

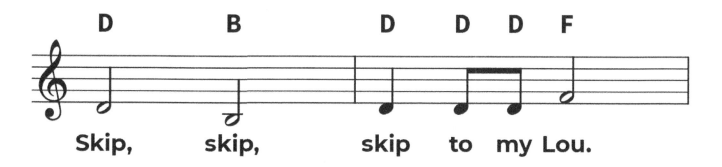

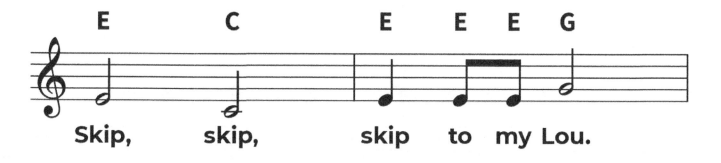

Scotland The Brave

C   C   D   E   C   E   G

Hark   when   the   night   is   fal - ling
There   were   the   hills   are   sleep-ing,

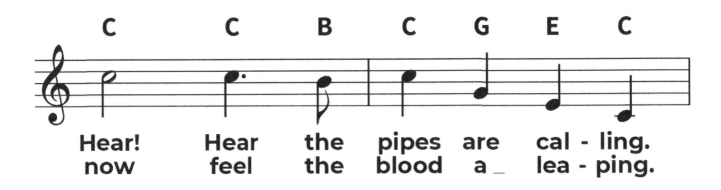

C   C   B   C   G   E   C

Hear!   Hear   the   pipes   are   cal - ling.
now   feel   the   blood   a _   lea - ping.

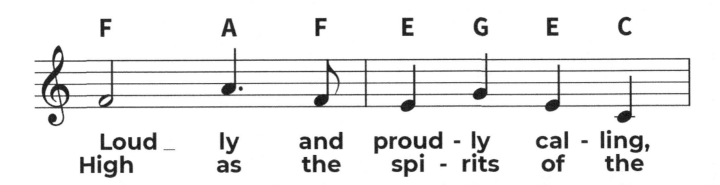

F   A   F   E   G   E   C

Loud _   ly   and   proud - ly   cal - ling,
High   as   the   spi - rits   of   the

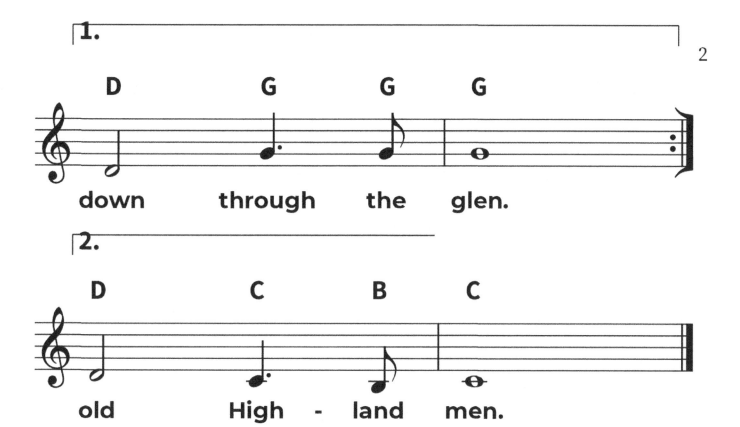

1.

D   G   G   G

down   through   the   glen.

2.

D   C   B   C

old   High - land   men.

Daisy Bell

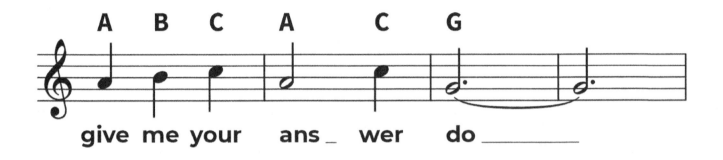

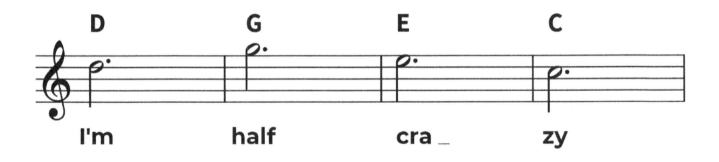

won't be a sty - lish mar - riage ____ I

can't af - ford a car - riage ____ But

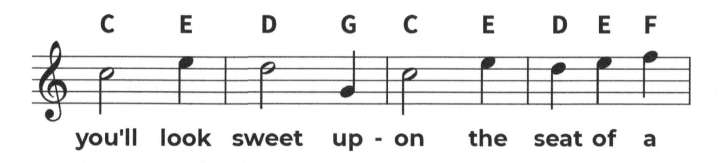

you'll look sweet up - on the seat of a

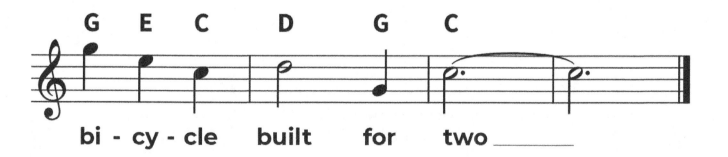

bi - cy - cle built for two _____

Baa Baa Black Sheep

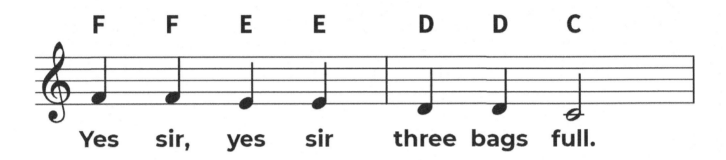

Jingle Bells

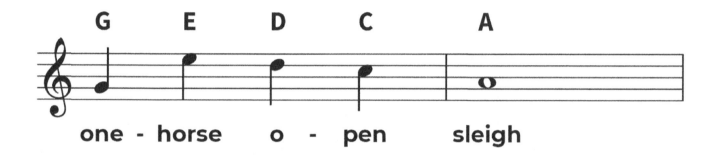

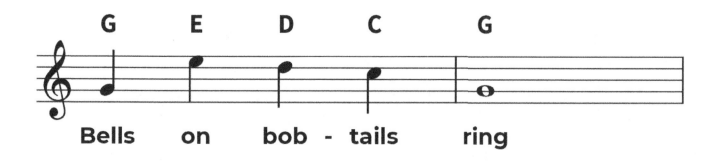

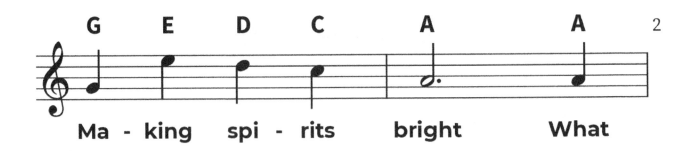

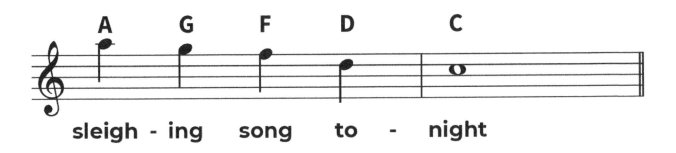

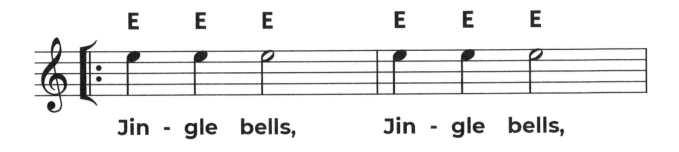

3

Oh, what fun it is to ride in a

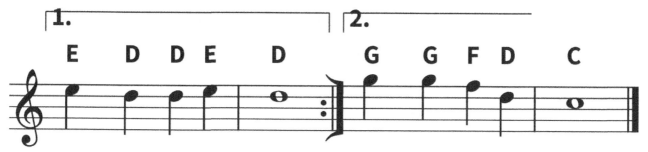

one-horse o-pen sleigh   one-horse o-pen sleigh

We Wish You a Merry Christmas

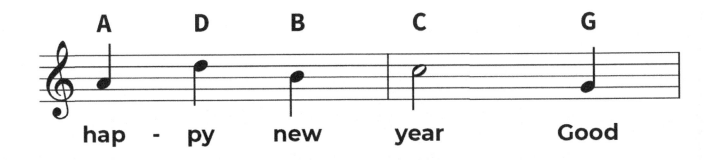

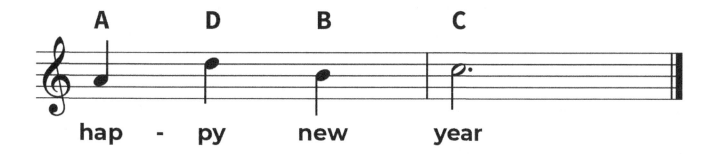

Girls and Boys Come Out to Play

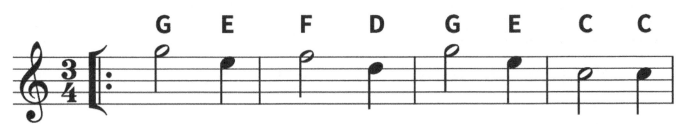

Here We Go Looby Loo

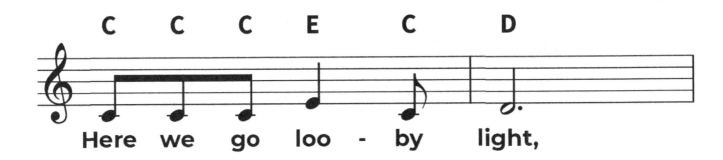

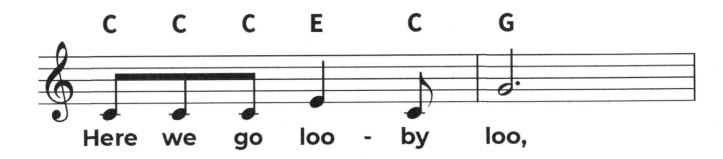

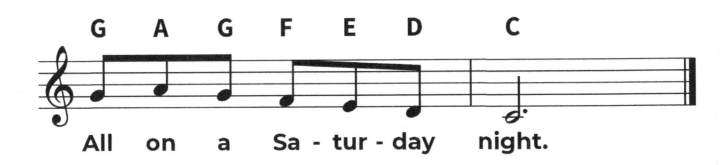

How to Play Piano
(A Crash Course For Complete Beginners)

First, let's take a look at the piano. Go ahead, play some keys. What do you notice?

Some keys are low like elephants stomping around.

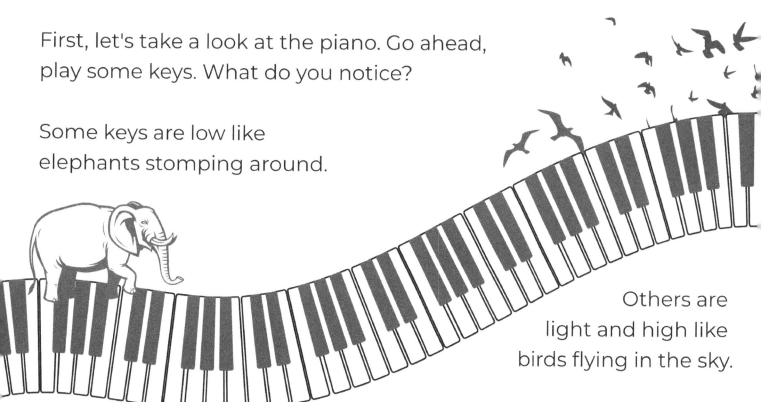

Others are light and high like birds flying in the sky.

Musicians write and read music in very much the same way as books. The lowest notes go at the very bottom, and the highest at the very top. Here are all the white notes, from the lowest (like the heavy elephant) to the highest (like the delicate bird).

The black dots (the **notes**) tell us what to play - whether it's high or low, fast or slow. They all hang from 5 lines like a washing line.

Those five lines are called the **staff.**

 At the beginning of every new line there's a beautiful spiral shape called the **treble clef**.

All the black notes are called **sharps.** They sound a bit strange, a bit sharp to our ears perhaps. When writing music we write sharps with a **#** sign next to them.

After the treble clef comes the **time signature**. Every piece of music has a beat, a rythm, that you tap your foot along to. The time signature has two numbers - the number at the top tells us how many beats will be in each bar and the bottom number tells us which kind of note we will be tapping our feet along to.

$$\frac{4}{4}$$

4 beats of 4th notes

$$\frac{3}{4}$$

3 beats of 4th notes

$$\frac{6}{8}$$

6 beats of 8th notes

$$\frac{3}{8}$$

3 beats of 8th notes

Enough about notation, how do you actually play on a piano?!

Ok, ok. Let's have a look at the piano. We already figured out that there's white and black notes, but look even closer. What pattern can you see?

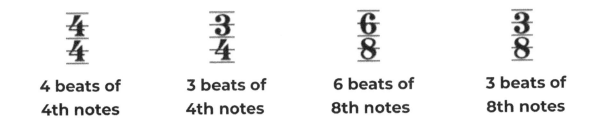

That's right! It's the same pattern again and again. 3 black keys, 2 black keys... again and again. These keys each have letters which are repeated along the entire length of the piano, called **octaves.**

So what are these notes?

Well let's start with the easiest ones to remember.

Find any two black keys. Notice how they look like two long ears of a dog? The note inbetween them is called the **D.**

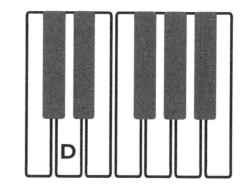

Next, find the 3 black notes. Put your finger on the one in the middle then slip it to the next white note higher up the piano. This is the first note of the alphabet - the **A.**

Guess what? The rest of the notes follow the alphabet, so **B** comes after **A**, **C** after **B**, and back to the **D.** Now we can fill in all the letters, all the way up to **G.**

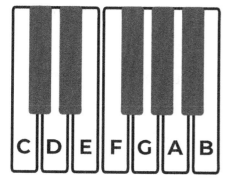

The sharps use the same letter as the white note to the left of them. So they look like this:

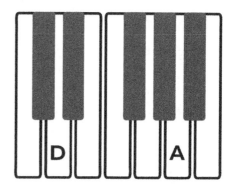

And voila! That's every single note on the piano!

The Notes

So now we know which notes to play, but for how long? Should they be quick and fast or long and slow? The type of note tells us how many beats to hold the key down for.

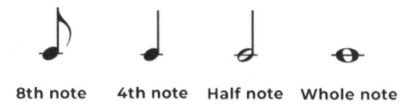

8th note   4th note   Half note   Whole note

A whole note is held down for twice as long as a half note, which is also the same as playing 4 quarter notes, or 8 eighth notes.

Sometimes we don't want to play anything! For these notes we rest and don't push any keys. In this book we will only use the quarter rest:

Dotted Notes

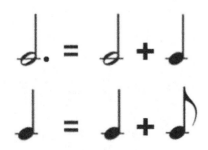

A dot after a note means that you should add half of the note to the note. So a dotted half note becomes a half + a quarter, and a dotted quarter becomes a quarter + an 8th.

The Repetitions

Sometimes we want to repeat certain parts of a song. Let's have a look at how we repeat different parts in piano sheet music.

Whenever you see these signs:

You can repeat everything within those brackets once. Like this:

Sometimes there's multiple parts to play, first to play one section and then the next section. In music notation these sections are labelled with 1 and 2 to tell you which parts to play first (first 1, then 2). Like this:

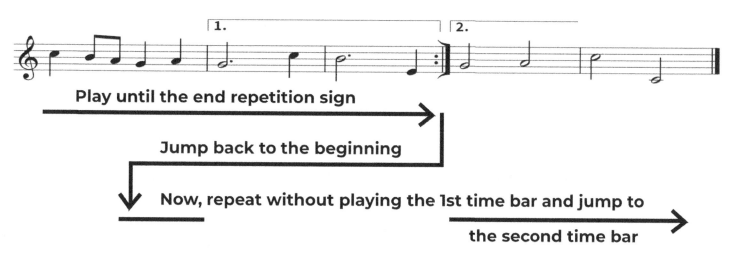

The Ties

In some songs you'll see some curved lines connecting notes together. They look a bit like skipping ropes or someone throwing a ball. They can also connect notes together across bars (over the fence). So when you see this symbol you should hold the key down until the second note is also finished - we add them together.

These tied 8th notes now last 2 beats

These tied half notes now last 4 beats

Ties can also work through bars. The half note last 3 beats now

And that's it! Now you know everything you need to read and play every song in this book.

The MP3 Files

Good news! For every song in this book we have given you the additional MP3 file so you can listen along and hear exactly how it is played on piano. We recommend listening to each song first to get an idea of the exact rythm and how it is played on piano.

To access all the audio files you can scan this QR code on your phone, or follow the link below. The files will be shared with you through GoogleDrive.

https://tinyurl.com/3tp9mnmf

If you have any questions at all, feel free to contact us through email
contactmontywebb@gmail.com

Write your own composition!

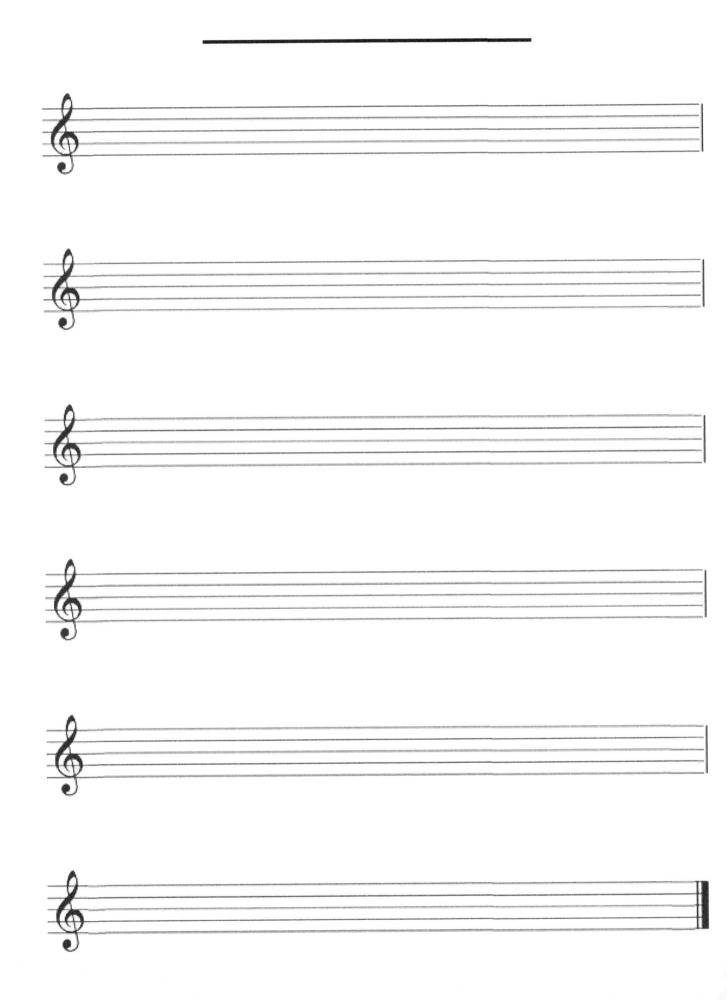

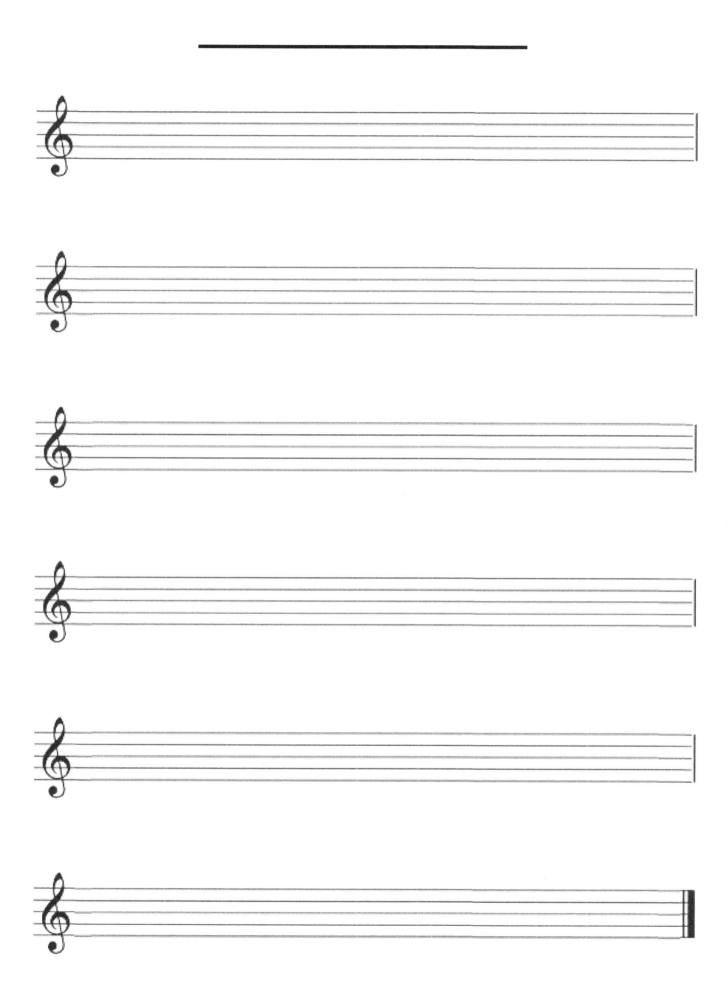

If you enjoyed this book please consider leaving us a **review on Amazon**. Leaving a review is the best thing you can do to support us - plus we just love reading your comments!

Amazon.com/review/create-review?
&asin=B09MYTMYTP

Thank you!

Other books by Monty Webb:

Made in the USA
Las Vegas, NV
21 October 2023